Message of Tears

Fr. Adolf Faroni, sdb

Printed and Distributed in the U.S.A. by:

101 Foundation, Inc.
PO Box 151
Asbury, NJ 08802

phone: (908) 689-8792
fax: (908) 689-1957

email: 101@101foundation.com
www.101foundation.com

ISBN: 1-890137-47-2

THE VIRGIN MARY IN TEARS
Why?

THE STATUE OF "ROSA MYSTICA"
IN TEARS
MAASMECHELEN, BELGIUM
AUGUST 8, 1983

CLARIFICATION

"In homage to the decrees of the Sacred Congregation of Rites, we declare that what is expressed in the present publication is to be given no other credence but the one which deserves a reliable human witness and that we, by no means, intend to hinder the judgment of the Holy Roman Catholic Church."

ACKNOWLEDGMENT

I wish to express my gratitude to the Magazine "IL SEGNO" which provided me with most of the material needed for this book; to Rev. Bro. Bernard and Mrs. Anita Gannon for their invaluable editorial work; and to all friends who have contributed to shouldering the expenses of printing and selling these books.

CONTENTS

The Statues of
 the Virgin Mary in Tears 6
Mary is Wounded 10
Lacrimation at Aci-San Filippo 15
Our Lady of the Rosary and
 the Sign of the Blood 19
She Just Cries! 41
Our Lady of Tears,
 Naju, South Korea 41
The Virgin Mary Appeared
 at Kibeho, Africa 44
The Rosa Mystica Shed Tears at
 Fontanelle in Montichiari
 Brescia, Italy 47
The Mystery of Akita........................... 49
The Bleeding on the Book "The
 Apparitions of the Virgin Mary" 57
Prodigious Lacrimation of the
 Virgin Mary at Syracuse.................. 61
The Sorrow of the Mother (Crosia) 67
Mary Shed Tears in Cameroon 69
Our Lady Speaks with Her Tears........ 75
Why Does the Virgin Mary Cry? 80
Tears of Sorrow, of Prayer, of Hope .. 86
Why the Virgin Mary Sheds Tears 94
Mary's Message 95
Our Lady's Request at Krushiv 96

THE STATUES OF THE VIRGIN MARY IN TEARS

We are witnesses of prodigious events in which the statues of the Virgin Mary shed tears. What meaning do we find in these events?

If the tears that these statues shed are real, are they a warning or an admonition? Why are they important to us? Are these tears of blood a sign of compassion for our wounded humanity?

Is it the sign of the times of a world doomed to destruction, fallen into evil, staggering in the dark, having lost the essence of truth and every hope? Is it to this wicked humanity that Jesus addressed these words in the Last Supper: "I do not pray for the world" (Jn 17,9)?

A chasm of confusion and corruption threatens the Church. The ministers of God are seduced by a new agnosticism, they have turned their back on the word of Christ and have become the cause of scandal. "I know that after my departure, savage wolves will come among you, and they will not spare the flock. And from your own group, men will come forward perverting the truth to draw the disciples away after them" (Acts 20,29-30).

Even before Paul, Jesus prophesied: "And then many will be led into sin, they will betray and hate one another. Many false prophets will arise and deceive many; and because of the increase of evildoing, the love of many will grow cold. But the one who perseveres to the end will be saved" (Mt 24, 10-13).

The twentieth century was full of wickedness. It was also full of apparitions of the Virgin Mary and of the Saints. The many apparitions of the Virgin Mary make true the vision of St. John: "A great sign appeared in the sky, a woman clothed with the sun, with the moon under her feet, and on her head a crown of twelve stars" (Rev. 12, 1).

In today's world, devastated by wars, plagues, earthquakes, sufferings, wickedness, tears, and blood, what meaning shall we give to the tears and blood that run on the face of the Blessed Virgin Mary? Is there a subtle relation among the Marian Prophecies?

In the La Salette message, the Virgin Mary announced to Maximin and Melanie that: "The earth will be struck by many kinds of plagues, wars. The seasons will change. The earth will produce bad fruits, the stars will lose their regular movement. The moon will reflect a reddish light. Earthquakes will destroy everything. Rome will lose its faith and will become the seat of the Antichrist."

In the third secret of Fatima, Our Lady announces: "There will be a great war in the second half of the twentieth century. Fire and smoke will fall from the sky. Millions and millions of men will perish and those who survive will envy the dead."

On the night of Holy Wednesday in 1969, a mystic, Teresa Musco, received the stigmata. Before dying at the age of 33, she had visions from the Virgin Mary who revealed to her the following: "My daughter, the punishment of the Heavenly Father on Italy is ready. You live in a difficult period in which everything is explained scientifically and there is no compassion for the poor... I wish to speak of the third secret of Fatima. It has been read long since, but no one has pronounced on it...because it is frightful..."

Lucia of Fatima gave some letters to Father Fuentes. Here are some extracts from the message published in the magazine *Immaculata* in 1959: "Many nations will disappear from the face of the earth, nations without God will be used by God to punish humanity. We are just in time to stop the punishment from Heaven ...each one on his own initiative, should perform good works, reform his life." She told me very clearly: "We are approaching the last days before the punishment. It is necessary to recognize this terrible reality."

The intention of this message is not to fill souls with fear, but to issue an urgent warning—a calling back to love and charity. The third secret of Fatima has a particular gravity confirmed by the tragic reality of today's world.

Are we truly at the end of time?

Let us read what Jesus answered to the apostles who questioned Him when all these things would take place. "What will be the sign of your coming and of the end of the world?" (Mt. 24,3).

He answered that there will be great plagues first: (Lk 21,11), earthquakes (Mt 24,7; Mk 13,8; Lk 21,11; Rev. 4,12-24 Lk 24, 7; Mk 13,8; Lk 21,11 Lk 21,25), wars and revolutions (Mt 24,6; Mk 13,7,8; Lk 21,9). All this is happening in the world. However, the greatest evil of the day is the loss of Faith. God is dead in the hearts of many men.

MARY IS WOUNDED

It was Tuesday, April 29, 1494, at 11:00 p.m. At that time, the day was divided into 24 hours as it is today, but the day would start at sunset. It was therefore considered early in the day. A certain John Zucano, nicknamed "Zuccone," was playing with his friend Comolo in the yard in front of the church dedicated to St. Mauritius. On the walls there was a painting of the "Madonna of the Milk," which is an image of the Blessed Virgin Mary feeding her Baby Jesus.

The game consisted of placing coins in a wooden pot. From some distance, one had to throw a stone scattering the coins around. Whoever succeeded in doing so was the winner.

The boy Zuccone had already lost many games and was losing all his coins, as well as his temper. Being terribly annoyed and in a fit of anger, he threw the stone not to the wooden pot, but to the painting of Our Lady on the wall. The stone hit the Blessed Virgin Mary right on Her forehead. His companion scolded him, and he, recognizing his wrong, knelt down begging for forgiveness. Then both of them, frightened, ran away.

Strange Prodigies

During the night, John of Miola from Re, and afterwards Anthony Ardicio from Craveggia, saw an unusual light under the porch as if it were from a lighted candle. They too were overtaken by fear and ran away.

Before sunrise, while opening the church for the ringing of the Angelus, the sacristan Steven from Gisla observed a woman, dressed in white, kneeling before the painted image. She seemed to him to be a lady who lived near his home. He greeted her as he did everyday, but he did not receive any answer. When he came out of the church, the woman had disappeared.

Finally the old man Bartholomew arrived, as usual, for his simple morning devotion. He touched the image of the Blessed Mother and kissed her hand. He realized with great surprise that it was wet with blood. His eyes, instinctively, turned towards the face of the Blessed Virgin Mary and he noticed the wound on the forehead, from which blood was trickling down.At once, he ran away and called the Rector of the Church, Fr. James. The bells were rung and heard, thus people came to church. The blood was falling to the ground and emanating a delicate perfume. The parish priest wiped it off with pieces of white cloth, which he later placed in a chalice.

The phenomenon lasted until May 18, intermittently, but always less abundant, as if the wound was healing gradually.

The Mayor of the place, Vigezzo Daniele Crespi, from Busto Sant'Arcizio, signed a parchment testifying to the events. It was also countersigned by four attorneys: Pierino Balconi, Giovannino Rossi, Pietro Rossi and Pietro Calconi.

The Event Repeated also in Bohemia

People planned the construction of a temple in honor of the "Our Lady of Blood." The devotion spread around Italy and through Europe. The most famous devotional image is the one taken to Bohemia at Klatovj by the chimney-sweeper Bartholomew Ricolgt who married a woman of that locality.

Before his death, he recommended to his daughter Anne that she have great veneration for the picture.

On July 8, 1685 Anne's husband, the tailor Andrea Hirshberg, suddenly saw a kind of perspiration tainted with blood coming out of the forehead of the Virgin Mary. The picture was at once taken to the church where a document testifying to the fact was drawn up and sent to the Bishop of Prague.

A Scientific Test

Today's man does not accept easily the truth of medieval documents, and this is also true in the case of the bleeding picture of the Blessed Virgin Mary. In 1962, Dr. Judica Cordiglia, from Turin, made a scientific investigation both on the blood relic and on the forehead of the fresco.

The result was astonishing. The spectrum showed the unmistakable elements of blood, and the rags used to wipe off the blood showed that they belong to the time of the miracle. The X-ray of the head of the Virgin Mary gives the evidence of a fracture of the frontal bone caused by something flat. The examination showed another fact, which escaped the perception of the witnesses at the time the events took place. The shedding of blood, rather than dripping straight down the smooth wall of the fresco, went along the contour of the face of the Virgin Mary and of the Child Jesus as if they were true live persons.

A Reflection

That a medieval picture should suddenly bleed itself is an impressive event. But that the painting should show the fracture of the head's bone, as in any real human being, is truly something much more than astonishing. This makes us believe in the miracle and the existence of a hidden Power that our science cannot explain.

The Mayor of the town, testifying to the events and the miracles, could not but help thinking that the event that took place would be an omen of misfortune. It is a thought that comes naturally even today, on witnessing the phenomena that have repeatedly happened in the last few years.

The Virgin Mary, Mother of Jesus was taken body and soul to Heaven and no stone can wound Her. If, therefore, God permits that a painting takes such reality as to be wounded, to bleed and then heal itself gradually, it is not to announce misfortune but to teach us how our actions have direct consequences, even though the damage is not immediately seen, as with Zuccone that night when he ran away. It is wrong to say that hurtful actions are just small sins. They may be more dangerous even though they seem to be of no importance, a mistake we often commit and perhaps do not confess. These sins hurt the Heart of Mary, which though assumed into Heaven, continues being vulnerable, because at the foot of the Cross, She accepted to be our Mother and She will suffer until we all reach salvation.

(Il Segno, Anno IV, N. 37)

LACRIMATION AT ACI-SAN FILIPPO

After the earthquakes that took place in Sicily in 1932, the attention of the people turned to the miraculous lacrimation of the statue of Our Lady. The phenomenon, which compelled the ecclesiastic authorities to intervene and examine, took place at Aci-San Filippo, a small center a few kilometers from Catania.

First, a photograph of the Blessed Virgin Immaculate exuded a kind of white ointment. Later, a statue of the Virgin Mary, one meter high, did the same. The statue, after being examined, was found to be normal, with no deceit, which prompted people to cry out, "a miracle!"

On October 7, 1987, narrates Antonio Pappalardo, twenty years old, "As I passed in front of the photograph that I had taken of the statue of the Virgin Mary, which is now kept in the parish church of my town, I realized that under Her eyes there were some stains. I looked at them attentively and to my great surprise, I noticed that it was blood. I was astonished. After a few moments, in the hope of being helped, I decided to inform Fr. Joseph Catalano, who for years had been the parish priest of my parish.

"Fr. Catalano," narrates Antonio, "came to my room in San Giuseppe St. He seemed skeptical. But after touching the Heart of the Virgin Mary, having his finger stained with red liquid, he realized that I was not imagining things nor telling lies.

"Following the advice of Fr. Catalano, I kept the greatest silence about the fact. A few days later, the news of the event spread and went beyond the boundaries of my small town. Involuntarily, it was the very same Fr. Catalano who betrayed himself by confiding to some faithful that a few steps away from the parish church, the Mother of Jesus was shedding tears of blood."

In view of the widespread concurrence

of the faithful in Pappalardo's house, with the intent of avoiding suspicion of deceit, the photo was soon sealed away.

In October 1987, in the presence of more than 200 persons, the Image of Mary was sealed off. The case seemed to be under control, but no more than six days later, in San Giuseppe St., forty-one people again cried out, "a miracle!"

The protagonist of the new inexplicable event this time was a statue of the Blessed Virgin Mary which Mr. Antonio, Giuseppe Pappalardo, had recently bought.

The first liquid came from the heart and feet of the statue. It seemed to me a kind of light ointment. Besides Fr. Catalano, the parish priest of the parish of the town of Ad Catena, Msgr. Di Santo, was also called. Both priests found no difficulty in recognizing the new perspiration. To avoid manifestations of fanaticism, it was decided to keep the greatest secrecy.

The repetition of the strange events, however, ended up making the event known. This moved the local press to give great importance to the event of the blood lacrimation, which for several years had been taking place in Catania, in the house of the visionary Maria Castorina.

Soon after this, the statue began to perspire blood, forcing Fr. Catalano and Msgr. Di Santo to take the necessary measures to guarantee the truthfulness of the lacrimation.

As they were not able to have incontrovertible witnesses from what was said by Fr, Antonio Pappalardo, the statue was sealed away. The two priests did this on December 4, 1988.

The statue of the Virgin Mary was enclosed in a crystal urn, with the small door sealed and signed by Fr. Catalano and Msgr. Di Santo.

Chemical Analysis

As the lacrimation persisted, and having being present at the repetition of the phenomenon, Mgsr. Salvatore Di Santo had the red liquid examined by chemical analysis. The result of the test forced the priest to declare: "the chemical analysis showed, with no doubt, that the samples given to the analyst contained clear traces of red blood cells."

Msgr. Di Santo asserted: "The other day, I personally noticed some drops falling from the mantle of the Virgin Mary. The drops of blood would gather at the foot of the statue and coagulate.

"I cannot pronounce myself," says the Parish Priest, "but I think that at this point, it is necessary to ask for an investigation. Many people attempting to appraise the Pappalardo family gave negative judgments, but in my opinion, it is a family whose honesty is beyond any doubt."

Having asked the ecclesiastical authorities to comment on this matter, Msgr. Salvatore Malandrino, bishop of Aci, decided not to oppose the future events in Pappalardo's house. "Pray and wait," said the Bishop, "God will enlighten us on the way."

A reflection is suggested by this event: The Blessed Virgin Mary is speaking to us by means of tears. She intended to warn us that our ways are getting further and further away from the way pointed out by Her Son two thousand years ago.

OUR LADY OF THE ROSARY AND THE SIGN OF THE BLOOD

The phenomenon of blood appearing on the picture of Our Lady of the Rosa in the house of the Attorney Cordiano Maropati, near Catania, Sicily, presents aspects that deserve our attention. Honest persons not inclined to believe easily in such kind of events witnessed the phenomenon of blood repeating itself.

The present information is given us by Father Alfonso and Msgr. Saverio Ferina.

People keep coming and visiting the Sacred Image. The room where the picture is kept is the destination of many pilgrims who, in addition to an innate inclination for the supernatural, feel the need of praying.

It is an undeniable fact that the event of the weeping picture had not deviated anyone from faith, rather it has been very useful to many in strengthening it.

The Blessed Virgin Mary is giving messages to a soul who calls herself "little Confidant of the Virgin Mary." She assures us that, long before she saw Virgin Mary shedding tears of blood, she received confidences of sorrow and bitterness for the grave offences done to Her Son Jesus. She was told on several occasions that those tears would manifest themselves visibly, and would leave visible signs.

The Little Confidant of the Virgin Mary admits that she can no longer keep silent because she received the order from the Virgin Mary to announce the Message to the whole world and in obedience to her confessor. Here is what she has entrusted us to transmit to the world in her name.

October 7, 1970

Mary said: "At this time, my daughter, in which I manifest myself with tears of blood, you should announce my will to your Spiritual Director and to the Bishop, as soon as possible.

"My beloved, I wish that my message be spread all over the world. Do not leave it in a corner. The lamp should not be placed under the table, but on the lampstand so that it may give light to everybody. it must reach every parish, and the whole world."

On December 8, 1970. as she often did, the little Confidant of the Blessed Virgin Mary was in prayer during a Holy Hour, when the Blessed Virgin Mary appeared and spoke to her:

"My little child, for years and months I have revealed to you that I shed true tears of blood...and have you seen the wounds on My knees?"

In fact, I saw the Blessed Mother many times kneeling down imploringly before the throne of God praying for sinful humanity.

"Men do not want to humble themselves, do not wish to convert themselves. It is necessary to pray and to pray much...dear little daughter, I announce to you that at Maropati in the house of Attorney Cordiano, I will shed abundant tears of blood from my image.

"Why?" the Confidant asked shyly. "I will relate the motives later," the Blessed Mother replied.

January 3, 1971:

At this point, the Confidant of Mary admits, with simplicity, to have been hesitant in the innermost of her soul, because she was profoundly convinced to be unworthy and too worthless a creature to receive such grace from the Blessed Virgin Mary.

"It is I, my daughter," the Holy Virgin Mary assured her, "and within a short time I will give you the proof. Believe Me, obey and pray with Me without ever growing tired. I bless you."

The proof came twenty-six days later, precisely on January 3, 1971, in the house of Attorney Cordiano in the town of Maropati. Abundant tears were seen flowing down from an image of the Virgin

Mary, which was hanging from the wall at the head of the bed. It stained the image with blood and then fell on the bed.

To dissipate any eventual doubt in the many hypothesis stirred by the phenomenon, now publicly known, which was also commented upon by the press, the Virgin Mary appeared to Her Confidant and told her: "My little daughter, what I told you I have said to no one... Do you understand? For years, I have told you to announce the coming of these events, and several times I told you to tell that it is truly the Virgin Mary who manifests herself in the house of Cordiano. They are truly My tears and they are tears of blood. I bless you."

In the meantime, the ecclesiastic authorities in their duty to keep the treasure of Faith intact and to divert the faithful from the danger of an easy religious exaltation, which could result in superstition, took interest on the phenomenon.

While in the house of Attorney Cordiano, the phenomenon repeated itself for some months, without the knowledge of any stranger, until unforeseen circumstances made it public. The Blessed Virgin Mary kept appearing and speaking to the

Confidant. On March 25, 1971, the Virgin Mary took care to reassure her Confidant, confirming what She had previously told her:

"My daughter, for sometime now I told you to tell the Bishop what I have revealed to you and to assure him that it is the Virgin Mary that is appearing...in the house of Attorney Cordiano. Tell him to believe without seeing and to have no doubt... They truly are My tears and tears of blood!"

"My daughter, in spite of all this, I am not able to placate the wrath of God. Pray and make others pray! I bless you."

May 8, 1971

While she was immersed in prayer asking for mercy upon sinful humanity, the Virgin Mary confided to her:

"My daughter, My tears of blood are not only for those who are far from God, but especially for the souls of religious and priests, because they are not what they should be..."

This time, Jesus was also present in the vision and He added to the Previous statement: "What mostly pains My Heart is the fall of the souls of religious and of priests, because they abandon their sublime vocation and draw many souls to hell..."

Then Our Lady resumed Her message: "They are tears, and they are tears of blood...tears of sorrow and of love which ask for a change of life because I wish all to be saved. I bless you."

To make the Confidant decide to include these words in the Message, the reassurance of the Virgin Mary was not enough. A formal command from her Spiritual Director was needed.

The tears of blood that fell on the wall under the picture of Our Lady of the Rosary, from simple drops of blood, stretched themselves to take the shape of a cross. Five are the crosses thus formed, and they are of different size.

June 13, 1971

Our Lady appeared to her Confidant and told her: "My daughter, the crosses which were formed on the wall represent the Crucifixion of My Son, which humanity renews in the five continents where He is continuously offended. I shed tears of blood because My Son is not loved. Prayer and penance! I bless you."

Also Miracles

While she was immersed in prayer, Our Lady appeared to her and told her: "My daughter, you must say to your Spiritual Director and to the bishop that in that house (where I shed tears), salvation will take place. There will also be miracles. I bless you together with the Bishop and your Spiritual Director."

On May 31, 1971, as she continued praying for sinful humanity, the Confidant of Mary saw Jesus in the Garden of Olives. Jesus was extremely sad. He was groaning and lamenting that sin pierced His Heart, and He repeated:

"I cannot bear any longer! I cannot bear any longer! They offend Me very much... I am trampled under foot daily, moment after moment. I wish reparation and to be loved! I wish love and reparation!"

"While I was praying," the Confidant of the Virgin Mary said, "I have seen the Virgin Mary in resplendent light, weeping and sorrowful. She told me: 'My daughter, at this moment, there are many who offend My Son! The world is in turmoil; the greater part of humanity no longer believes. The priests are no longer as they should be. Look at My Son, how they have trampled Him underfoot and they continue doing so...'"

At this point, the Confidant saw Jesus down on the ground. He was leaning on His elbows. His Adorable Head was crowned with thorns and was bleeding. The weeping Virgin Mary lifted Him up and pressed Him to Her breast and said: "Make amends, make amends! I can bear it no longer!"

The Confidant of Mary, at that sight, remained deeply grieved and said, with her broken heart, "Oh my Jesus, how I have trampled upon you!" and Jesus: "Not you, but the greatest part of humanity."

"What can I do to make amends?" asks the Confidant, and Jesus: "I will tell you during the Holy Hour."

In fact, on the First Friday of June, while the Confidant of Mary was passing the nightly Holy Hour, she had a vision:

"I saw the Heart of Jesus in a dazzling light. It was a miracle I was not blinded by it. Jesus was sad and sorrowful and called me: 'Spouse, obey, you will tell My Vicar that I can no longer bear it. I am continuously offended and trampled upon, I am much offended, today more than in the past. What a pain! I have told you many times that what mostly afflicts My heart is the fall of religious souls and of priests. They abandon their lofty vocation and draw many souls to hell. The others!... My altars... Reparation! Reparation! Many and many sins are committed in the world. The first and the greatest of My commandments is trampled upon. Very few are the souls that truly love Me. I wish love and atonement. I wish it above all from My Vicar, from My bishops, and from My priests...'"

The Virgin Mary appeared to her: "It is I, dear daughter, much prayer is needed, nightly prayer from all the clergy and the laity. We should hold the atoning Holy Hour at night from 11:00 to 12:00. It is the hour in which My Son is mostly offended. We should pray much to keep the divine punishment away and for the conversion of the world. Let us pray, My daughter, that this plague of sin which floods the whole world may cease. Let us incessantly pray and do penance! Otherwise, not much time will pass before the destruction of the whole of humanity. Daughter, let us pray together, never grow tired of it. I bless you."

On another day, the Virgin Mary insisting on the same theme, said: "You must announce that this Message is the motherly warning of the Mother of God to humanity today more than ever disoriented by the present evil.

"I wish all to be saved, and I am shedding tears of blood for everybody. But if humanity does not cooperate, it will be terribly punished, and My tears will be shed in vain. It is urgent. They should be aware of this terrible reality. It is time for everyone to perform holy works and reform his own life according to the warnings Jesus has given together with those of the Virgin Mary."

September 8, 1971

The Blessed Virgin Mary appeared to Her Confidant and told her:

"I am Our Lady of the Rosary of the Tears of Blood. My daughter, you should tell the Bishop and your Spiritual Director that it is not a ghost or a magic phenomenon, but it is My true blood, shed and mixed with the blood of Jesus. I repeat, My daughter, they must do their best to build a Shrine. For the time being, let them turn the rooms into a chapel."

September 12, 1971

While the Confidant of the Virgin Mary was deep in prayer, Mary confided to her: "My daughter, God is Love! And this love is requited by humanity with ingratitude, scorn, even with calumnies. For this purpose, I pray continuously before the throne of God and I shed tears of blood. My Son wants to be loved and not trampled upon, He is continuously derided, My daughter...there is no second without Him being offended and crucified." The Confidant relates, "I heard these words pronounced in a heartrending voice... I could see abundant tears of blood falling down from the Virgin Mary's eyes. The vision of that blood and the pain of Our Lady pierced my heart and I fainted. On recovering consciousness, I heard Our Lady saying: 'My daughter: love, atonement, prayer. I bless you!'"

September 15, 1971.

"I continued to pray, and I saw Jesus Crucified. He told me: 'I am again truly crucified, My suffering has increased, My wounds are deeper. I am not obeyed!... In My name, all the faithful should be one single heart and soul. Instead, not even among the consecrated souls is there union and charity. They say they have to adapt themselves to the times...yet My law never changes!...My words will never fail! What I have always said, I confirm. My law does not change, they should keep it...observe it!'

"The Blessed Virgin Mary remarked: 'Poor Bishops...they will not know what to do, how to solve so many problems!'"

October 7, 1971

"Among other things, the Virgin Mary wishes that the Rosary be recited with love and devotion, every day in the place where She shed tears and in the families, according to her intention. One should add to the Rosary this prayer: 'Our Lady of the Rosary of the Tears of Blood, pray for us and for the whole world.'"

The Rosary

"Since the time when the Virgin Mary gave great importance to the Rosary, there are neither material nor spiritual problems that cannot be solved with the help of the Holy Rosary and with the sacrifices offered for Christ and with Christ. Reciting it with love and devotion, Mary will be consoled and many tears of Her Immaculate Heart will be wiped away. The Blessed Virgin

Mary said it many a time. On the same day, while I was deep in prayer, the Virgin Mary said:

"'My dear little daughter, by order of your Spouse Jesus and of His Celestial Mother, on the 15th of the month, you should go to the Bishop and tell him what I have revealed to you and what I wish. I bless you.'"

December 8, 1971

While the Confidant of Mary was deep in prayer, the voice of Jesus was heard: "There are those who insult Me who put My image underfoot. After Holy Mass, they cause Me pain..."

On the same occasion while praying, the Blessed Mother was heard saying: "The third part of humanity hates one another and kills one another. Pray with Me, daughter, without ever growing tired, so that men may find the way to union in charity and into one single fold under one Shepherd only.

"Much blood is shed by humanity. Day after day, thousands and thousands of men die. These are divine punishments. Men ought to realize that these scourges and these punishments will fall on them if they do not reform themselves. We are still in time to stop punishment from Heaven. What is needed to avert it is incessant prayer! Penance! I bless you."

May 8, 1972

The Confidant of the Virgin Mary, during her nightly adoration, had the vision of the Blessed Mother who told her:

"My daughter, what I have told you for years, I repeat again. I wish that all Priests have their nightly Holy Hour on the first Saturday of the month, with a spirit of penance, according to my intention. In addition, I wish that all priests commit themselves to form in every parish a group of prayerful and atoning souls—victim hosts—Eucharistic souls—who will offer everything for love to the Divine Heart of Jesus, through My Immaculate Heart according to My intention...unceasing prayer and peace! My daughter, I bless you."

May 31, 1972

The "Little Confidant of Mary" was deep in prayer. With a loud voice, the Virgin Mary called her: "My daughter, My daughter, I announce to you a message always old and always new. The message that years ago, by order of Jesus, you have sent to the Pope, should be announced to the whole world. It is the message of charity, to love God!...to love the neighbor!...

"It is the message that My Son brought to the earth and has announced to the world with His word but above all with His works...the message of charity. It is the message of messages... Unique... Supreme ... Eternal!...on which the Gospels are based...and the work of God... Creation... Redemption... Paradise! ...God is love! and has loved men unto death...and this love is reciprocated with offenses and ingratitude... My Son wishes to be loved by all, because He has shed His blood for all. He wishes it especially from the souls of religious and priests, and from all those who profess themselves to be Christian. My Son is not loved and for this reason, I shed tears of blood! My daughter, I bless you."

May 31, 1972

While the Confidant of Mary continued her nocturnal prayer, Mary appeared. She told her in a compelling manner: "My dear daughter, in My name, you have to tell what I have told you for years... I wish all priests to have a way of life worthy of their lofty vocation...let them wake up...let them work with zeal like the first apostles, for the glory of God and the good of souls.

"I wish them to be carriers of truth, of charity, and of grace and not of scandals!... There are many, daughter... One should pray and pray much. Unceasing prayer from all, and penance! I bless you."

October 7, 1972

The Confidant of Mary narrated: "While I was immersed in prayer, at a certain moment, I felt that my spirit was taken away by a mysterious supernatural power. Soon after, the Virgin Mary appeared to me radiant in light. Gradually the light became stronger and I saw a great table, and on it a Tabernacle on it with these words written in gold:

This is the Great Treasure

Mystery of Love!

Source of Salvation

Fount of Eternal Life

"The Virgin Mary pointed with Her hand to the Tabernacle and told me: 'The Eucharist, Fount of Salvation, Fount of Eternal Life! God is in the midst of men but men do not appreciate Him because they do not know Him and those who know Him are for the most part indifferent...'

"Suddenly, the door of the Tabernacle opened and I saw a Host, coming out, great, radiant in light and a host of angels surrounding It.

"Immediately after, instead of the Host, I saw Jesus in person Who, with a finger of His right hand, was pointing at His Adorable Heart, saying: 'Behold that Heart that has loved men so much...and in exchange of such great love, they offend Me greatly, day after day, moment after moment.'

"At this point, Mary intervened: 'Daughter, the greatest part of humanity is thirsty for what the world cannot give...it is dazed by modern wickedness, satisfies its thirst at the poisonous fount of evil. And their souls are the victims of sin.'

"With a forceful voice, She said to me: 'I wish that everybody great and small, receive Holy Communion frequently and with due dispositions, the Eucharist, "Fount of Salvation" and of "Eternal Life," so that one may live in the Grace of God, and in eternal life.'

"Further, the Virgin Mary wishes that the Priests commit themselves with faith and love, to make souls know the greatness and importance of the Eucharist, "Fount of Salvation," inviting souls to receive Holy Communion often and with devotion.

"The Mother of God repeated again with compelling voice, 'I wish that everybody, big and small, go to the Sacrament of Penance and of the Eucharist: only thus the kingdom of God on earth will hasten.'

"'The Eucharist saves souls!

"'The Eucharist makes saints!

"'I wish the salvation of the whole world. For everybody, I shed tears of Blood... But if humanity does not correspond, it will be terribly punished. Pray, daughter, without ever getting tired and make people pray that souls may be saved and God may be loved and glorified eternally. I bless you.'"

August 15, 1972

Our Lady said to the Confidant in explicit terms: "If humanity does not listen and believe in His words, there will come a plague which will destroy three fourths of humanity."

Mary's Confidant, as usual, continued her nightly prayer. With simplicity, she admits: "As I was praying, I had a vision. I saw a great round table representing the world. Jesus was at the center, radiant with light. He had the aspect of a young, tall, and most handsome youth whose enchanting beauty cannot be told... On the table there was all kinds of food, and Jesus was lovingly distributing it to a multitude of men, women, and all the while, the food did not lessen but it increased more and more.

"As I continued to pray, soon after, I saw another large table, the Eucharistic banquet. Jesus was at its center in a resplendent light and there was a multitude of angels all around. He Himself, with a great ciborium in His hands, was distributing Holy Communion.

"The voice of Jesus said: 'My dear children, behold here I am for you. Take and eat, this is My Body. Take and drink, this is My Blood, which I shed for you and for all.'

"Soon after, at the center of the two tables, I saw Jesus Crucified, whose size was from earth to Heaven. The multitude that before had their fill at the table prepared by Him, was furious with Him and threw stones at the Cross. They hit

Him with spears, spitting and jeering. Then I saw His Adorable Body dripping blood from head to foot.

"At this sight, I felt my heart was breaking with pain. Such was the pain I experienced that I fainted and fell on the floor. Miraculously, I did not die.

"Coming around after a short time, I saw the Blessed Virgin Mary, very sad and in great pain at the foot of Jesus Crucified. Weeping and imploring, She was looking at Her Son Jesus, and I saw in Her face abundant tears of blood.

"With an anguished voice, She told me: 'You see, My daughter, how the love of My Son is reciprocated...the third part of humanity offends Him and continuously tramples upon Him, day after day, moment after moment. One part of them is composed of religious...but they do not want to convert themselves, one should pray much.' With a compelling voice, the Blessed Virgin Mary exclaimed: 'Come, come all of you to My Son! He will give you peace, love, salvation.'

"All of a sudden, I saw Jesus, Who turned to the crowd and said: 'What wrong have I done to you? I have fed you, I have prepared a table for your body and your soul, for the length of your life. I have given all of Myself, I have shed all My blood for you... What more could I have done?'

"The Blessed Virgin Mary intervened and said: 'Oh soul redeemed by the Blood of Christ, think well on this and decide to love Jesus who loves you so much, unto folly.'

"The voice of Jesus: 'In spite of your ingratitude, I continue to love you and through My Heavenly Mother, I embrace you all. My spouse, I bless you.'

While I was still praying, I had another vision: I saw the Blessed Mother as large as from earth to Heaven which means that Mary is the Mediatrix between God and man.

At the same time, I saw Jesus in the heavens with open arms. He was embracing the whole world. A great number of angels were surrounding a multitude of men, women and children of every age crying out: 'Hosanna! Hosanna! ...in the highest Heaven!' And the Virgin Mary was saying: 'Come, come all of you to My Son, He is ready to forgive you, to give you peace and salvation.'"

SHE JUST CRIES!

"Here we cannot breath for the air is polluted by the exaltation of sin: abortions publicly held with great demonstrations helped by the police, homosexuals...a bold sexuality, infantile pornography. The Virgin Mary presented Herself in new forms. In many places where there is a statue, it often sheds human tears during Holy Mass: they are silent tears, without messages, as if one having suffered too much has no more words to say. The newspapers speak of it sometimes disrespectfully, other times in a perplexed manner..."

(Johanne Ellis, Washington)

OUR LADY OF TEARS, NAJU, SOUTH KOREA

Julia Kim, the visionary from Naju, writes: "At about 8 in the morning, I heard the Virgin Mary calling me. I went to the room functioning as a chapel, where there was the statue, which had already shed so many tears. (Our Lady cried for 700 days, from June 30, 1985 to January 14, 1992).

"The Virgin Mary was smiling and seemed to be more beautiful than ever. In fact, the face of the Virgin Mary did not stop expressing Her sentiments, which the pilgrims could witness. I fell into a profound meditation, when suddenly, the place where I was on my knees, was pervaded by a powerful light.

I looked up and I noticed that the light was surrounding the statue of Our Lady, and that there were two most beautiful angels, one at the right and the other at the left side of Mary. Suddenly, the statue of the Virgin Mary changed into a beautiful and living being. Then, I heard Her telling me with a tender and amiable voice:

"'My dear daughter! How many tears I have shed; tears of blood for 700 days. (The Vocabulary of Mystical Theology says regarding numbers: number 7 suggests a considerable number, 70 a number even superior to it, and 700 suggests the plenitude of it.)

Also, I have shown on My head My perfumed oil for 400 days. (Number four signifies the totality of the geographical horizon, front, back, right and left side.)

"'In the meantime, allowing a period of preparation, with all My Love, I let flow My perfumed oil from My whole body for the salvation of My children in this world, for 700 days until the present day.

And yet, how many of My children have come back to me?

"'Oh My daughter! I can wash Myself alone, or let Me be washed by My angels, but I ask you to wash Me with the water I have prepared for you. (Our Lady refers here to the "spring of water," which She pointed out to Julia on the mountain chosen by Her.)

"'And now I wish that all My children console Me and surround Me with their devotion and dedication, with their sincere hearts, with their love full of filial piety. Oh My daughter! You see how the world, where evil and sin are ever growing, is facing threats and is in constant danger.

"'It is necessary therefore that you hasten to announce, exercising the spirit of martyrdom, the will of this Mother in anguish to the children of the whole world, in a last and supreme attempt to save humanity in this so grave an hour in which the cup of the wrath of God is overflowing.

"'At present, humanity is going through painful hours. In the Church, apostasy and infidelity are developing alarmingly as the result of the work of Free Masonry. Many ecclesiastics and religious neglect their vocation, and as they are spiritually blind and deaf, they see and understand nothing because of their inner corruptions. Oh, how My Motherly Heart is in pain!

"'When you shall live a consecrated life, make sacrifices and penances for the conversion and salvation of My children, I will guide you through a safe way to lead you all to Heaven.'"

THE VIRGIN MARY APPEARED AT KIBEHO, AFRICA

The Bishop of Butare, in Rwanda, has approved an apparition of Our Lady that took place in Kibeho, a small village in his diocese in the center of Africa.

Rwanda is one of the smallest countries of Africa, inhabited by 7 million people. The first evangelization there took place a little more than 100 years ago. In 1895, the first group of people were baptized at Save, a village near Kibeho. From the very start, the missionaries consecrated the mission to the Sacred Heart of Jesus. The two first priests were ordained in 1917 and the first two native religious took the religious habit in 1914. Today, Catholics comprise 50% of the population, Protestants—20%, and the rest continue with their traditional belief. The Virgin Mary has appeared in this country, which is among the poorest of the world. On the night of November 28, 1981, Alphonsine, 15-years-old, and two of her companions, who were guests in a poor school directed by European and native sisters, went for a walk to the top of a small hill near the school.

All of a sudden, Alphonsine saw a great light, similar to a luminous cloud coming towards her from above. She knelt and out of fear closed her eyes.

Later, Alphonsine said, "At that moment, I felt a great peace and a profound joy in my heart. I opened my eyes and I saw a most beautiful Lady dressed in white with the Rosary in Her hands."

A few days later, three other girls of the village had the same vision at different times. Shortly after that, a boy, Segatasha, a pagan, completely ignorant of the faith and of the Catholic Church, saw Jesus dressed like a shepherd. Jesus Himself revealed to him who He was and in a few days instructed him in the Faith. The parish priest and the Bishop were astonished to see that this pagan boy knew everything about faith, especially since he knew not how to read and write.

In the meantime, the Blessed Virgin Mary continued appearing to the shepherd girls and to the boy at different intervals individually and in tears.

The apparitions of the Virgin Mary ended at the end of 1983, with the exception of Alphonsine who continued seeing the Blessed Mother every November 28th. In the meantime, the boy was baptized with the name of Immanuel.

The message delivered by the Virgin Mary is the same as all those given by the Blessed Mother: prayer (especially the Rosary), conversion of the heart, fasting, reconciliation among tribes, Christian renewal, the conversion of pagans and Protestants, holiness of the priests and religious. The new element of these messages was: "Be missionaries of charity towards the poor, share everything, be brothers to everybody."

In the message of 1983, the Virgin Mary told Anatalie: "Sins are more numerous than the drops of water in the sea, the world is drifting towards its ruin."

Alphonsine saw the Mother of God in tears. The visionaries cried, shivered, and gnashed their teeth. Many times during the visions, which lasted about eight hours, they felt crushed by the weight of their bodies. It was in the apparition of August 19, 1982, that the visionaries saw terrifying images: a river of blood, people killing one another, corpses abandoned, trees in flames, the opening of an abyss, a monster, decapitated bodies. The people present on that day were about 20,000 and all felt the sense of fear, of terror, and of sadness.

On November 1986, on the hill of the apparitions, there were many faithful in prayer. Alphonsine was there in ecstasy for more than one hour. Over the loud speaker, people were listening to the words directed by the seer to the Virgin Mary, but those of the Virgin Mary could not be heard. At the end of the vision, two big tears appeared on the face of Alphonsine.

The Virgin Mary presented herself with the most beautiful title we can give Her: MOTHER OF THE WORD MADE FLESH.

THE ROSA MYSTICA SHED TEARS AT FONTANELLE IN MONTICHIARI BRESCIA, ITALY

It happened on Sunday, September 2, 1990 at 11:00 a.m. Thirty persons were praying in front and around the small statue of the Virgin Mary that stands above a pool of water, which people, in good and bad health, submerged in while asking for graces. Some were barefooted in the water.

A lady from Milan was kneeling down in the pool of water, under the statue. As she lifted her eyes, she realized that the face of the Virgin Mary was marked with tears. At once, she told those present who did not realize what was happening. Bewildered and touched by the fact, they knelt down in prayer and all prayed together.

The tears were descending from the right eye while the left one was only veiled. She shed tears until midday.

Among the pilgrims, there was one from Brescia, Angela Tirelli, who for two years had come to the place begging Mary for the grace of being cured from a severe ailment in her ears. Three days after her return home, she smelt a nice perfume. As she thought it was coming from roses outside, she opened the window and at once she felt totally cured!

The other spectacular event besides the shedding of tears was the face of Mary in tears. A pilgrim present during the lacrimation photographed Her.

The statue is of modest height (74 cm, 80 cm with the base) and is made of the material with which statues are made today. She has blue eyes with the white pupils slightly turned downward. She shows no particular expression. In the photo, one notices Her shining eyes with tears, while from the left eye, some tears are trickling down the cheek. The face is no longer the one of a statue, but has become a human face. It is the soft face of a woman, as if it were a living person, with the sad eyes of a person who is crying. All the while, the neck was unchanged, and remained as it was sculptured.

Why did the Rosa Mystica shed tears at Fontanelle? If Mary is crying, the reason must be very grave. Every person should search within himself for the reason for these tears.

THE MYSTERY OF AKITA

In Akita, Japan, an unusual event made the 115 million Japanese think and wonder at what caught the attention of the press and television.

Every continent seems to have its own Medjugorje. What is happening? Never like today have we had so many supernatural manifestations, and especially in places completely unknown such as Akita in Japan, diocese of Niigata. There are approximately 400,000 Catholics in Japan.

The small convent of the Institute of the Servants of the Eucharist, is a hymn to poverty. Part of the small chapel was built with material taken from an old poultry house. For about 4 to 5 months a year, those who inhabit the convent, besides the lack of comfort, are buried under snow. They lead a difficult kind of life.

The extraordinary events began on June 12, 1973. For three consecutive days, Sister Agnes Sasagawa Katsuko observed luminous rays coming from the Tabernacle of the chapel.

On June 24, Corpus Christi, the luminous rays were more resplendent still.

On June 28, eve of the Feast of the Sacred Heart, a wound in the shape of a rather large cross, appeared on the palm of the left hand of Agnes.

A similar wound appeared on July 6, 1973 on the right hand of the statue of the Virgin Mary. Blood began dripping from that wound in the shape of a cross. The phenomenon repeated several times.

On Friday, June 29, Feast of the Sacred Heart, angels appeared around the altar singing the "Holy, Holy, Holy."

On Friday, July 6, at about 3:00 a.m., a lady appeared to Sister Agnes saying: "Do not fear, I am the one who is near you and takes care of you, follow me." Only later did the sister understoand who she was—it was her Guardian Angel who had taken on the semblance of her deceased sister.

The angel said: "Do not fear, pray for your sins but also in reparation for all the sins of humanity. The present world wounds the Sacred Heart with its ingratitude and offenses. The wound in the hand of the Blessed Virgin Mary is much deeper than yours. Let us now go together to the chapel..."

When they arrived there, the angel disappeared. Sister Agnes found herself in adoration before the Tabernacle. Then she approached the statue of the Virgin Mary to check the depth of Our Lady's wound.

A sweet and mysterious voice came from the image made of wood. "My daughter, My novice, you have obeyed well by detaching yourself from everything. Does the illness of your deafness make you suffer? You will be cured from it! (a thing that took place in two period of times). Be patient. It is the last trial. Does the wound on your hand give you pain?

"Pray in atonement for all men. All the girls who are here, taken one by one are as precious to Me as the pupil of My eye... Pray much for the Pope, bishops, and priests... Continue praying much... Speak to your Superior of what I have told you today, and do what she tells you."

On July 25, the founder of the Institute, Msgr. Ito, Bishop of the Diocese of Niigata, came to the convent. He followed the event of presumed supernatural origin. He remained in the place during the duration of the event, and he approved it at the end of a serious investigation.

On July 26, blood of dark color came out abundantly from the hand of the statue. On the next day, the excruciating pain in the hand of sister Agnes came to an end. It was foretold by the angel.

A Message for the World

On August 3, the voice of the Virgin Mary was heard as She gave the second message to Sister Agnes:

"If you love the Lord, listen attentively. What I am about to tell you is important, and you will transmit it to your superior. Many people in the world offend the Lord. I need people who console Him. My Son and I wish souls who may atone with their suffering and their poverty for the sins and for those who are ungrateful, in order to placate the wrath of the Heavenly Father. To make you understand how much the Father is irritated with this world, He is determined to allow a great punishment to fall on the whole of humanity."

The message in its final part anticipates the benevolence of the superior towards the events, and the obstacles placed by the first commission of studies against the apparitions that have really taken place.

Unceasing perspiration, lacrimation, abundant shedding of blood, ineffable perfumes characterized the statue of the Virgin Mary of Akita.

On October 13, 1973 a mysterious light pervaded the whole chapel, while coming from the statue, a perfume beyond description filled the place.

The Blessed Virgin Mary was there to give the third message, the most important of all: "As I have announced previously, if men will not convert themselves, the Father will let a great punishment fall on the whole human race.

"Without doubt, it will be a terrible punishment, greater than the Deluge, such as has never been seen till now.

"Fire will fall from Heaven. Because of this punishment, a great part of humanity will perish. The priest will die with the faithful. The men who will be spared will know such sufferings that will make them envy the dead. The only weapon remaining will be the Rosary and the Sign given by My Son. Recite the Rosary daily! With this devotion, pray for bishops and priests. The action of Satan has penetrated also inside the Church. The cardinals will go against cardinals, the bishops against bishops. The priests who will honor Me will be despised, offended, fought against by their own confreres. The altar, the church will be ransacked. The Church will be filled with persons that are compromised. By the action of the demon, many priests and religious will abandon their vocation (it is what has happened in these last years).

"The demon will enrage especially against those who have offered themselves to the Father. The loss of many souls is the cause of My pain. If sin continues to be committed and goes beyond the present measure, also the forgiveness of sin will disappear."

Many theologians have refused to accept this message. However, the documentation of Akita reached the Vatican in 1982.

The catastrophic and grave message is not a new one, perhaps it is a confirmation of the previous ones. Mystics, prophets, and visionaries from many parts of the world have said the same things. The worst, however, is always avoidable, as our Lady of Medjugorje has said. At Kibeho and in other places such as Akita, Mary points out the solution through the prayer of the heart, affirming that this can stop any natural calamity as well as the hand of God who is about to strike us!

Therefore, they are not messages of fear, but compelling messages due to the gravity of the situation.

In fact, towards the end of the third message, hope remained in Sister Agnes: "Recite many Rosaries. I alone still can save you from the evils that are announced. He who trusts in Me will be saved."

October 13, 1974

Sister Agnes was instantly cured from her deafness. The benefit lasted six months.

And then, on the last Sunday of the month of May 1982, the promise of the Virgin Mary had its complete fulfillment. Sister Agnes recovered her hearing permanently on Pentecost day.

On January 4, 1975, the statue of the Virgin of Akita shed abundant tears.

Bishop Ito, Teiji Yasuda (chaplain and spiritual director of the visionary) and Father Joseph Marie Jacq (from whom we received the detailed information on Akita) were witnesses several times of the event, which the angel interpreted this way: "Do not be astonished to see the Virgin Mary crying. One soul only which is converted is precious to Her Heart. She manifests Her sorrow to revive your faith, so inclined to weaken.

There were 101 lacrimations until September 15, 1981.

The local medical tests of the university of Akita and of GIFU have proven that it is the case of true human perspiration, human tears, and blood type O.

Bishop Ito recognized as supernatural the events of Akita through a long message, read in the churches during Holy Mass on Easter Sunday, April 22, 1984.

On February 15, 1950, the Virgin Mary, through a consecrated soul, promised that "Japan will be converted!"

THE BLEEDING ON THE BOOK "THE APPARITIONS OF THE VIRGIN MARY"

Sunday, December 4, 1994.

The periodical ABC published a surprising article titled: "A picture of the Virgin Mary, printed on a book titled *The Apparitions of Our Lady*, bleeds publicly."

Due to the unusual event of bleeding in a book, although we should not be surprised of anything in the history of Mysticisms, for the absolute truth of the facts, we came to know and we questioned all the witnesses involved in the case. Because we sincerely believe that such heavenly manifestations do not take place to be kept secret, we feel morally and spiritually obliged to divulge the facts.

The two-page article, shows a photo of the visionary of Pedrera, Carmen Lopez, and the book *Apparitions of the Virgin Mary*, opened on page 136. In the book is found the picture of Mary, the "Mystical Rose," which shed tears of blood, a phenomenon which had taken place on September 15, 1984 in Columbia, and which had caused a great sensation as well as wide skepticism.

The current supernatural event took place on the morning of August 6, 1994 inside the very modest house of Carmen, a construction known as "El Higueron." That night, about 200 persons were praying the Rosary outside the house. People continued coming to the place because of the prodigies that often took place there.

Carmen, half unconscious in her room, at the request of the Virgin Mary, was looking for the book already mentioned, which opened on page 136 where, as we said, there was the picture of the Rosa Mystica.

Immediately, on the same bleeding tears of the photo, authentic blood appeared clearly visible to all people.

The author of the book by name of Speranza Ridruejo, was there on this occasion. She took the book and went out to show the picture to everybody present. At the same time, all those who were present sensed an indescribable perfume of roses.

After a few days, Speranza went again to El Higueron accompanied by two doctors and by a friend of hers, who was at that time the Italian Ambassador to Spain. On opening the book with the intention of taking photos, she noticed that tears began forming in the eyes of the Virgin Mary. They were tears of blood of the size of lentils, which began to grow at the sight of everybody. In this second lacrimation, the tears filtrated and stained several pages of the book.

On August 13, along with several other persons, Dr. Sergio Triay from Gibraltar went to the house. Upon his request, the visionary Carmen showed him the book which she keep carefully enclosed in a crystal urn. The Doctor's declaration was that it was "human blood, alive and recently shed."

Later, another lacrimation, the third one, took place according to information recently received as follows:

The book of Pitita Ridruejo bleeds for the third time.

The book, The Apparitions of the Virgin Mary was in a crystal urn, which was locked. At Pedrera, last January 16, at 9:40 p.m., the visionary Carmen Lopez fell into ecstasy and continued bleeding abundantly from the cross on her forehead, from the thorns of the head and of the heart. At the same time, the reproduction of the "Christ of Limpias," which she kept in her prayer room, and which had bled several other times, started bleeding visibly in the presence of all. "No more blood, no more blood, no!" she cried out before all the witnesses. At the same time, the book of Pitita Redruejo was bleeding.

The important fact here is that the moment of bleeding coincided with the time in which the earthquake of Kobe took place. This indicates that disasters such as wars are a punishment from Heaven, as are earthquakes, tidal waves, plagues, incurable illnesses, atmospheric manifestations, and the convulsive reactions of nature. These are all permitted by the Creator of the Universe, God.

The fact of the coincidence of the earthquake and the bleeding invites us to reflect.

PRODIGIOUS LACRIMATION OF THE VIRGIN MARY AT SYRACUSE

No doubt, remarks Pope Pius XII, Mary is in Heaven and She is certainly happy. She suffers neither pain nor sadness. Yet She does not remain insensitive, rather She always has love and pity for this miserable humanity to whom She was given as Mother, since the time when sorrowful and tearful, She stood at the foot of the Cross where Her Son was crucified.

Will men understand the mysterious meaning of these tears? Oh, the tears of the Blessed Virgin Mary! They were, on Mount Golgotha, tears of pity for Her Son Jesus and of sadness for the sins of men.

Does She cry today for the renewed wounds caused to the Mystical Body of Christ? Or are they tears waiting for the return of Her children who were faithful in the past and who now are seduced to join the ranks of the enemies of God?

In my opinion, no one could have given a more authoritative explanation of the four days of Mary's tears at Syracuse, relating them to the death of Jesus on Mount Golgotha, than Pope Pius XII.

The Tears of Mary

"From the very beginning of that day, August 29, 1953, as soon as I came to know that a ceramic statue of the Virgin Mary, representing Her Immaculate Heart, was shedding tears in Orti street, I hastened to leave my parish and go to the place of the prodigy.

"Through the help of a policeman, I managed to enter the room, and sitting on the bed, I was able to see the picture of Our Lady, which at that moment was shedding tears. I felt a great emotion, which increased when Mrs. Giusto allowed me to take the picture in my hands and present it to the multitude outside the window.

"The face of the Virgin Mary was stained with tears, which were running down Her cheek and along Her mantle, and filled the right hand, which was touching Her small Heart.

"Another moment of emotion for me was when I dared touch the tears with my small finger, and I soaked a piece of silk cloth offered to me by my sister.

"The greatest emotion of my heart was when I tasted one tear from the Virgin Mary's eyes. What moments! What untold anxiety! Those tears had the very taste of tears. It was the greatest gift Mary could give me... I felt something overwhelmingly sweet and tremendous which shook me. I shivered all over. I was not the only one to taste those tears. I remember that an Officer with fifty policemen were there to protect the small picture of the Blessed Mother. They were witnesses of the miraculous lacrimation. It is impossible to describe the anxiety of those who saw the Icon shedding tears, and which continued to shed tears at intervals, and confirmed the reality of Her tears.

"I saw communists, masons, and Protestants who were bewildered in the presence of the evidence of the prodigy, and made the sign of the cross and prayed. Everybody was praying.

"On the second day of lacrimation, the picture was no longer there. I learned from the Commissary Ferrigno that it was brought to the police station. It was here that in the presence of the husband of Mrs. Giusto, the picture was taken out of the glass case, carefully examined and found to be completely dry. This inspection was repeated by the doctors before the analysis of the tears, to which I was a witness. Thus it excluded any danger of deceit. Later, it was placed above the arc at the entrance of the house of Mrs. Giusto, to be seen by all people."

The crowd kept coming and observing the tears of the Virgin Mary.

On October 1, a chemical commission from the Provincial Office of Hygiene and Prophylaxis, by order of the Archbishop, collected a cubic centimeter of tears, which was then submitted to all kinds of tests. Chemical reactive test were performed on the microscope and humid procedure test were directly observed as well as being dried on the oxygen flame.

The result of the test and analysis, given by Prof. Leopoldo La Rosa, was the following: "We have had the express reaction P.H. 6,9. The liquid coming from the eyes of the Image of Our Lady has the analogous composition of human tears."

It was then that the Archbishop of Syracuse, Msgr. Ettore Baranzini, accompanied by the Metropolitan Chapter, the Mayor, the Prefect, the Judge, and by all the other authorities went to Orti Street for his first encounter with the Blessed Mother.

The Canonical trial

On the evening of September 19, the Archbishop, accompanied by all the authorities, returned the picture, which was placed in an artistic reliquary and put in Piazza Euripides to make it easier for the faithful to see the image.

It was necessary to initiate a canonical trial organized by the Ecclesiastic Tribunal, to gather the testimony of the thousands of witnesses.

In May, 1954, on the occasion of the fiftieth anniversary of priesthood of the Archbishop, all the Bishops of Sicily gathered in Piazza Euripides. It was the first procession with the picture of Our Lady carried in triumph in an artistic golden reliquary decorated with rare gems. The reliquary contained the crystallized tears of Our Lady together with wads soaked in the tears of the Blessed Mother. The next day, the Archbishop laid the first stone of the magnificent shrine, which has since been completed.

Thus it was, that the silent message of the tears of the Blessed Virgin Mary, renewed for four days in this city, was like a light on top of the tower of a boat on the rough sea of this century.

Silent tears, without word, without a sigh, without a sob, because when the heart of a Mother is not listened to, nothing remains to Her but to shed tears for the salvation of Her children. We know well the message of Fatima, in 1917, in which the vision of hell was also shown.

Tears! Behold the last message of the Sorrowful Heart of a Mother, the Mother of Jesus. Tears! The most powerful weapon of children when the word dies in the heart and melts in tears, and it is the weapon of the great ones when sorrow closes their lips.

Thus, in Syracuse, the Virgin Mary did not appear with a message. She did not speak. She just cried from a small picture, from such a humble image, from a piece of chalk, on the bed of a young mother afflicted by suffering.

True tears, human, touched, photographed, collected, tasting similar to our tears. Innocent tears! Warm tears of a Divine Mother who is begging Her children to abandon the ways of sin and perdition. Tears which are retained in Her Heart, and which have the bitter taste of all the sins of the world.

And I always ask myself, who will ever

be able to evaluate the tears of a Mother, and of such a Mother, whom Jesus dying on the cross left to us as the last testament of His love; Mary, the spiritual Mother of humanity in the order of grace and of redemption?

Behold, therefore, how after Fatima, the tears of the Virgin Mary are for me and for you undoubtedly the strongest and most prodigious supernatural sign. They remind us of those tears She shed at the foot of the Cross, at Rue du Bac in Paris, under the eyes of Catherine Labouré, at La Salette before Maximin and Melanie, and at Lourdes before Bernardette.

Pray much and you will better understand the language of tears of the Blessed Virgin Mary, our Mother.

THE SORROW OF THE MOTHER (CROSIA)

A prophetic message on August 9, 1994 sheds more light on the recent lacrimation of the statues of the Blessed Virgin Mary in the world.

Anna Biasi, the visionary, narrates the following:

"I was half awaken and, due to reasons which I could not explain, my soul continuously impelled me to turn my thought to God.

"All of a sudden, three flashes of lightning called me to an unexpected reality. First, I saw a luminous globe which was advancing towards me, then from it, I saw the bursting out of that light of paradise which is now familiar to me, the Virgin Mary. The Celestial Mother Mary sat on my bed.

"I did not greet Her because Her aspect was profoundly sad. After the first words of blessing, She began crying. She announced: 'I am your Sorrowful Mother.' Then She began to describe Her pain which deeply affected my soul.

"She cried during the whole apparition and I with Her. She cried with sobs when She spoke of the Church, of the Pope, of the souls who are failing into hell, of the lack of understanding on the part of bishops, priests and faithful...

"She said: 'Great is My grief seeing the Pope yielding under the weight of a most heavy cross, while being misunderstood, he is surrounded by the indifference of the bishops, priests, and faithful! This, My beloved son, much loved by My Son Jesus, finds himself praying and suffering under the Cross. He loves much and lives with the Church. He suffers for those who are in war.'

"In the midst of much incredulity regarding Her manifestations, accompanied by Graces and Miracles here in Crosia, and though witnessed by Her children, She is being continuously wounded. Always under the cross of each one of us, She exhorts us to wake up and to understand that we all are under the threat of war, and the tragic echo reaches our ears!

"'My children, never like the present time, have I been so near to you, to speak to you for so longer a time!'

"With this last expression of Her Motherly Love, She exhorts us to accept the invitation to eternal salvation, telling us:

"'Pray, pray with true love, and open yourselves up to Jesus, who is forgiveness.'

"She disappeared, She kissed me as I was left in tears."

MARY SHED TEARS IN CAMEROON

The Bishop of Obala spoke to his faithful about the statue of the Blessed Virgin Mary that shed tears in the office of Father Paul Noma Bikibili. Here is the text of the pastoral exhortation of August 19, 1994, from Msgr. Jerome Owono Mimbol to the faithful of Obala:

"Some news has been spread recently throughout the diocese regarding the statue of Our Lady which has shed tears in the office of one of my young priest, Father Paul Noma Bikibili, at Obala. Since several hundred people of every walk of life, according to Father Noma Bikibili, have seen this unusual event, and also because the radio and the national television have spread the news through interviews and photos of it, the news has spread beyond the parish "Mary Mother of God," and even beyond the diocese of Obala. These facts force me to speak.

"To those belonging to my Diocese, who impatiently question the facts and who are anxious to know the thought and behavior of their Bishop, I wish to tell them what their Bishop thinks:

"Dear children, Father Paul Noma informed me by telephone of the phenomenon that took place in his office, when he saw that the statue of the Virgin Mary, placed on a shelf was shedding tears. This phenomenon repeated itself for many days. Further Father Paul Noma Bikibili has sent me a written document which contains the necessary information about the phenomena observed and the message given to him.

"However, I think that the faithful of my diocese did not need to wait for such manifestation to give themselves to a sincere devotion of the Virgin Mary, Patroness of Cameroon and of the diocese of Obala.

"To the faithful of Christ in the Diocese of Obala, I say: Yes, the Virgin Mary cries. If she did not cry at Obala, she has already cried somewhere else. And if She did cry at Obala, she will cry again elsewhere.

"Yes, the Virgin Mary cries when She sees the Christians, Her children and for whom Christ has died, abandon the true Church in order to embrace sects and satanic cults.

"Yes, The Virgin Mary cries, it is true, at the increase of criminality in Cameroon. People steal for a radio or a transistor, and kill a father in front of his wife and children. Houses are ransacked, cars are stolen. No crime seems to be grave enough at present.

"Human life has no more value though God has died for men at a high price.

Brothers kill for a piece of land; the sons kill their parents because of controversy. The depravation of customs is such that truth, justice, honesty, purity seem to be banned from our society, and have given free rein to unrestrained ambition and a limitless greed.

"Yes, Our Lady cries when homicides are organized in Cameroon and in the world as a result of abortion, without the Human Rights Organization intervening and reacting as they do in many other cases.

"The Virgin Mary cries, and cannot but cry, at seeing corruption becoming a system which controls the activities of the entire society. Injustice reigns as a law which oppresses the poor, the widows and the orphans above all.

"We are a humanity of sinners. The Virgin Mary cries at seeing that we do not want to convert ourselves, to change life, to do penance. To my children of the diocese of Obala, I say that the Virgin Mary cries because of our sins and our hardness of heart. And if She cries at Obala it is, no doubt, to give again a warning, not only to the faithful of Obala but to all the Christians and to all people of good will."

"Here is the message that Father Paul Noma Bikibili declared to have received from the one who presented herself under the title of the 'Blessed Mother:'

"'I ask men to pray, to pray much for the whole world. I have already prayed for it to My Son, but men do not seem to be willing to be converted, and they continuously do evil things. My Son is angry with the whole world. He says He is about to abandon the earth. He says He has already sent many messengers to men to invite them to conversion, but in vain. He says He has given them time to be converted, to change life, but to no avail. What should I do? I am already tired of interceding. This is why I cry, tears of love, My Motherly tears fall down! I am asking men to be converted. I am asking them to pray much for the whole world, so that men may convert.

"'As my tears are shed in Cameroon, this message is particularly addressed to the inhabitants of Cameroon. I am the Blessed Mother.'

"I therefore invite the faithful of the Diocese of Obala to avoid any useless unrest. However, the skeptics will not fail to oppose the message as will those who will make it a mockery. But all should know that an apparition is not a dogma of faith. It depends first of all on personal devotion. It is not necessary to have a public and official cult. In any case, the Church, in these cases, prefers to take time and act with prudence.

"With or without extraordinary manifestations, each one should double his ardor in prayer and in his devotion to the Blessed Mother. Everyone is invited to deepen his own faith. All must accept the need of converting themselves, to pray, to make penance to obtain forgiveness from the merciful Heart of Jesus and the grace of conversion for everybody. This is what was and is the most important thing, and which the Church never ceases to recommend with insistence in the liturgical periods of Advent, of Lent and in all other occasions.

The Spiritual Significance of the Phenomenon

"If the Blessed Virgin Mary did not cry at Obala, she has already cried somewhere else. And if she had cried at Obola, she will cry elsewhere." With these balanced words, Msgr. Jerome Owono Mimboe tried to solve the enigma of the apparition of the crying Virgin Mary witnessed by one of his priests.

At every apparition of Jesus and Mary, those responsible for the running of the Catholic Church usually show an initial skepticism which is a methodical doubt. Initially, they refuse to believe, but in their hearts, all clerics must harbor a certain desire to see the official recognition of an apparition.

The Bishop of Obala finds himself in a dilemma: he must safeguard the truth of faith, but at the same time, he must guard himself from opposing the faith of the faithful. He must act with prudence and with a rationality often not understood.

He, therefore, cannot for the time being confirm the truth of the supernatural facts witnessed by a priest, but he cannot invalidate them either. Furthermore, he can no longer keep silence and he affirms: "Yes, the Virgin Mary is crying." (From *l'Effort Camerounais*)

OUR LADY SPEAKS WITH HER TEARS

The tears of Our Lady of Syracuse move us to ask a question: Why? Why did Mary cry? She did not speak as She did to Catherine Labouré, as in Lourdes to Bernardette, or as in Fatima to the three Portuguese children. She just cried, but how eloquent are those tears!

Crying is the language of sorrow. When a mother cries, it is a sign that she has exhausted all arguments to lead Her children back to the right path.

At Fatima, She renewed Her appeal inviting to penance and prayer for the conversion of sinners. At Syracuse, She just cried, She shed tears.

Father Jozo, who saw Our Lady at Medjugorje, speaking on this theme of "The Tears of the Virgin Mary," shared these thoughts: "The Blessed Virgin Mary cries with visible tears. It is a strong impression to see the Virgin Mary crying. I have seen Her while She was crying. It is no fun to say that the Virgin Mary is crying. It is a responsibility to say that the Virgin Mary sheds tears like rain. Those tears wish to purify our land, to purify our mentality..."

No law can modify a reality of nature, which is the will of God. Father Jozo has also spoken of one of his recent encounters with His Holiness, Pope John Paul II in the Vatican: "He clasped me strongly by the hand and wanted to know everything about Medjugorje. He said: 'You should protect Medjugorje.'"

At Civitavecchia, the Virgin Mary in tears has spoken with so much eloquence without speaking. What the theologians find hard to explain, the heart of those who love God find easy to understand.

There is no doubt that the solicitous and sorrowful Mother shed tears with the desire and hope preventing those tears from being ours in a future not too far off. Perhaps Her tears are one of Her attempts to stop the shedding of blood, no longer of Her Son... but of Her children.

"Our Lady shed tears," Cardinal Schuster wrote regarding Syracuse, "because a relevant number of Catholics ignore the Gospel and do not live in the Spirit of Christ any longer. They materialize their own faith into such traditional forms that have little influence on their moral conduct.

Mary shed tears also because among consecrated souls, many have not yet understood the gravity of the hour and are very little concerned with the need of reforming their lives and the lives of the Christian people entrusted to them.

Our Lady also cries because the world does not pray. Men no longer know how to pray because they are proud and do not bend their foreheads to God nor invoke the Holy Spirit. The world believes and trusts in men, it does not believe and trust in God.

Jesus said to Valtorta (1/7/43): "By telling Abraham to find ten just people, I did not intend to say that a place is saved where ten just men are found. But we can understand without error that if ten just and generous souls gather for prayer, with a holy end to ask for help for the place, I will not reject their prayer. Have I not said that I will listen to the prayers done by a group of persons gathered in My name? My words and promises do not fail. But will the persons who gather for prayer be constant in faith, sacrifice, spiritual purity, and in the singleness of intention? However, if they are true priests—and those who pray and give themselves up for the brethren are true priests—I will bless them and I will give them what is asked in My name."

The Lord said to the visionary Luisa Piccaretta: "It is true that great will be the suffering, but know that I will have consideration for the souls and places where there are souls who do My will."

There is no doubt that the Virgin Mary has not cried in vain. There are already conversions, and there will be still more.

The Virgin Mary told Maria Rinaldi: "I have cried for the desolation that will come upon you. But," She added, "do not fear, though terror will sweep the whole earth, yet where I have appeared in these last years it was with the intention to put a beam of protection against the enemy who is encircling you."

The Blessed Virgin Mary has appeared often in these last times and many of us fear that a supernatural apparition might bring signs of punishments from God, or catastrophes.

It is strange, though, that the Blessed Virgin Mary appears shedding tears when She is in divine happiness.

This means that when She appears, She is not indifferent towards us. As a Mother, She cannot be indifferent to our sorrows.

There are two voices among the visionaries of Medjugorje. Some, like Mirjana, say that the punishment will not be changed. Other seers of Medjugorje say that prayer and fasting can suspend even the natural laws and cataclysms.

I have asked several times why some of you say that prayer and fasting can change events? I think that the punishment cannot change because men do not want to change. Men are those who should change. Those who reformed themselves have caused a change in the seventh secret given to the visionaries in Medjugorje.

I think that all this may be interpreted more in the sense of hope than in the sense of a catastrophe. All the seers agree that, though there is something grave in store for the world, nevertheless if we are with God, in the Love of God, all will be well, because we cannot lose the love of God, it will develop even in the last trial.

WHY DOES THE VIRGIN MARY CRY?

In the morning of August 6, 1987, on the feast of the Transfiguration, Father Jozo Zovko, who was parish priest of Medjugorje at the time when the apparitions started, concelebrated a long and beautiful Holy Mass. On this occasion, he spoke of the five times in which the Virgin Mary was seen crying by the visionaries during six years of apparitions. Here are his words, which coming from him who suffered imprisonment for the sake of the faith, take on a special value:

"The Virgin Mary has explained, at Medjugorje, the mystery of Holy Mass. I speak of this because there are so many priests here in this concelebration. We cannot know the mystery of the Holy Mass because we stay so short a time on our knees before the Blessed Sacrament. We are not able to celebrate and live the Holy Mass because we have no time to prepare ourselves for it and no time to give thanks after it. We are not able to pray because we are busy and we have much work: we have no time to pray. This is why we are not able to live the Holy Mass.

"I wish to tell you how the Virgin Mary thinks: The Virgin Mary taught us how to climb the mountain where Holy Mass is lived, where our death, our resurrection, our change, our transfiguration take place.

"Our Lady said: 'You are not able to live the Holy Mass, and She began to cry. Our Lady did not cry much. Our Lady cried four times only and recently once again. She cried was when She spoke about us priests; when She spoke on the

Bible; when She spoke on Holy Mass; then She cried when She spoke on peace a week before Gorbachev and Reagan met at Reykjavik to try a way to make peace; and recently, She cried again when She gave a great message for the youth about a month ago.

"When Our Lady spoke of Holy Mass, She shed tears. Why? We have lost a fundamental thing: the Church, in many of her faithful, has lost the value of Holy Mass."

At this, point Father Jozo spoke of Jesus' tears at the tomb of Lazarus, saying that Jesus cried because not one of those present, knew who He was. The sisters of Lazarus, and the very apostles who had been with Him for three years, had not understood who He was. "Do you not know me?" We do the same today in Holy Mass: we do not recognize Jesus.

"The Blessed Virgin Mary is sad to see you and me at Holy Mass. She cried! And I feel how in the tears of the Virgin Mary, your heart can melt even if it were made of stone; how your life, which is spoiled and ruined, can melt and be cured.

"Our Lady does not cry for petty matters. When Our Lady cries, her tears are heavy. Very heavy indeed. And they are powerful. They are capable of opening whatever is closed. Before crying, Our Lady first put a question: 'Why do you not know how to live Holy Mass?'"

Then Father Jozo took them back to the Last Supper in spirit, to make them live that first Eucharistic celebration. He added:

"Our Lady said: 'He who does not read the Bible cannot pray, does not know how to pray. He who is not able to live the Holy Mass, is not able to live. He who is not capable of making sacrifices, to practice self-denial and fast, is not able to live Holy Mass; cannot feel the sacrifice of Holy Mass and other sacrifices...'"

At this point, the question come back which we often hear: how can the Blessed Virgin Mary cry if She is living the glory of paradise, rejoicing in the beatific vision of God?

The answer is not easy because we deal with eternity and we are still prisoners of time. For this reason, we can only understand up to a certain extent. Besides, notwithstanding some clear interventions of the pontifical magisterium, there are today theological tendencies which deny that Christ, during His earthly lifetime, had the beatific vision: consequently He would not have had a perfect rapport with his Father! This is not a safe conclusion because Jesus is always God.

These theologians say: as Christ had suffered, was hungry, and died, it is impossible that these sufferings be true if He continued enjoying the beatific vision.

Hence, He had to abandon the beatific vision.

Today this continues: if it is true that the Virgin Mary is sad, if it is true that Christ when He appeared to Mary Margaret Alacoque and to many other mystics was sad, and so, when He showed his wounds to St. Catherine of Siena and others, then we would be facing something that is false. Let us therefore ask for enlightenment from the pontifical magisterium.

In the recent Encyclical on the Holy Spirit, the Holy Father recalls to mind the traditional doctrine of the Church: that is, the Church, "The Mystical Body," is the continuation of the incarnation of Christ in His earthly body. Therefore, with our sins, we are the wounds of Christ, and Christ suffers in the Church.

This is very important because it also explains why the Virgin Mary is asking for penance. Why is She sad? She is sad because of our sins, because our sins make the Mystical Body of Christ truly suffer, through the Church.

Therefore, it is true that Christ and Mary are in Heaven, in eternity; but history, up to now, is not yet completed in as much as They live through the Mystical Body of the Church and the whole suffering of humanity until the end. There is no contradiction. The doctrine of those theologians put in danger the Divinity of Christ.

We all experience that in life, there can be joy and sadness at the same time. Our Lady intervenes to remind us, that with sin, we make the Mystical Body of Christ, the Church, suffer. Thus we understand the stigmata in some saints as Padre Pio. The wounds of Christ in their body remind us that this is provoked by our sins. The saints, because of their sanctity, continue to carry the wounds of Christ more deeply in their flesh, because they are the ones who save us. Every sin of ours continues to nail Christ in His own "Mystical Body" in the Church. For this reason, we would do well to do penance and be converted to obtain, already in this present life, the benefits of peace, of joy and of serenity.

TEARS OF SORROW, OF PRAYER, OF HOPE

"As He drew near, He saw the city and wept over it." (Lk 19,41)

There was a place in Jerusalem, on the side of the Mount of Olives, where according to tradition, Christ wept over the city of Jerusalem. In those tears of the Son of Man, there is almost a distant echo of other tears, of which the first reading taken from the book of Nehemiah tells us.

After the return from the Babylonian slavery, the Israelites set themselves to rebuild the Temple. First, however, they listened to the words of Sacred Scripture and of the priest Esdra, who at the end, blessed the people with the book of the Law. Then all burst into tears. In fact, we read that the governor Nehemiah and the priest Esdra told them: "This day is consecrated to the Lord your God. Do not mourn and do not cry! Do not grow sad, because the joy of the Lord is your strength" (Ne 8,9,10).

The Israelites' tears were tears of joy

for the recovery of the temple, and for the conquered liberty.

The cry of Christ on the side of the Mount of Olives was not a cry of joy. In fact, He exclaimed:

"Jerusalem, Jerusalem, you who kill the prophets and stone those sent to you, how many times I yearned to gather your children together, as a hen gathers her young under her wings, but you were unwilling! Behold, your house will be abandoned, desolate. I tell you, you will not see Me again until you say, 'Blessed is He who comes in the name of the Lord.'" The Lord will later say similar words on the way to Calvary when meeting the weeping women of Jerusalem.

Jesus' tears over Jerusalem express His love for the Eternal City. At the same time, they manifest His sadness for the near tragic future, which He foresees: the city will be conquered and the Temple destroyed, the young will suffer the same torture, death on the cross. "At that time people will say to the mountains, 'Fall upon us!' and to the hills, 'Cover us!' For if these things are done when the wood is green, what will happen when it is dry?" (Lk 23, 30-31).

We know that Jesus cried another time, at the tomb of Lazarus. "'See how He loved him!' But some of them said, 'Could not the one who opened the eyes of the blind man have done something so that this man would not have died?' (Jn 11, 36-37).

"So Jesus, moved with tears, came to the tomb. He gave the order to take away the stone, and raising His eyes to the Father, He cried out in a loud voice, 'Lazarus come out!'" (Jn 11,38-43).

The Gospel tells us again of the feelings of Jesus, when moved by the Holy Spirit cried out: "I give You praise, Father, Lord of Heaven and earth; for although You have hidden these things from the wise and the learned, You have revealed them to the childlike. Yes, Father, such has been Your gracious will" (Lk 10,2 1). Jesus rejoices for the Divine Paternity. He rejoices because it is granted Him to reveal this paternity, and finally rejoices for a particular irradiation of this paternity on the small ones.

The Evangelist Luke defines all this as rejoicing in the Holy Spirit. An exaltation which moves Jesus to reveal himself still more: "All things have been handed over by My Father, and no one knows who the Son is except the Father, and who the Father is except the Son, and anyone to whom the Son wishes to reveal Him" (Lk 10, 2 1).

In the Cenacle, Jesus foretells the Apostles their future, crying: "Amen, amen, I say to you, you will weep and mourn, while the world rejoices; you will grieve, but your grief will become joy." And He added: "When a woman is in labor, she is in anguish because her hour has arrived; but when she has given birth to a child, she no longer remembers the pain because of her joy that a child has been born into the world" (Jn 16, 20-21). Thus Jesus speaks of the sadness and the joy of the Church, of its crying and its joy, referring to the image of a woman who gives birth."

The evangelical narration never tells of the tears of the Blessed Virgin Mary. We do not hear Mary weeping on Mount Golgotha when She was at the foot of the Cross. Neither are we given the chance to know Her tears of joy when Christ rose from the dead.

Though Holy Scripture does not mention this fact, yet the intuition of faith speaks in favor of this. Mary crying in pain and joy is the expression of the Church, which rejoices on Christmas night, suffers on Good Friday at the foot of the Cross, and again rejoices at the dawn of Resurrection. She is the spouse of the Lamb, which is presented by the second reading of the Apocalypse (Ct. Ap. 21,9).

The tears of Mary are seen in apparitions when She, from time to time, accompanies the Church along the roads of the world. Mary cried at La Salette, in the middle of the last century, before the apparitions of Lourdes, in a period in which France showed a growing hostility to Christianity.

She cried again at Syracuse, at the conclusion of the Second World War. It is possible to understand those tears in the background of those tragic events: the immense massacre provoked by the conflict, the extermination of the children of Israel, the threat to Europe coming from the East, by the professed atheistic Communism.

Also the Virgin Mary of Czestochowa shed tears at Lublin—a fact little known outside Poland. Instead, the event of Syracuse is very well known and many are the pilgrims who went and still go there.

Cardinal Stefan Wyszynski came to Syracuse on pilgrimage, in 1957, after being liberated from prison:

"I myself, being at the time a young Bishop, have come here during the Council and I was able to celebrate Holy Mass on All Souls Day."

"The tears of Our Lady belong to the order of signs. They witness to the presence of the Mother in the Church and in the world. A mother cries when she sees her children threatened by some spiritual or material evil. Mary shed tears, sharing in the weeping of Jesus over Jerusalem, by the sepulcher of Lazarus or on the Way of the Cross.

"We should also remember the tears of Peter. The Gospel narrates the confession of Peter, near Cesarea Philippi. We listen to the words of Christ: 'Blessed are you, Simon son of Jonah. For flesh and blood have not revealed this to you, but My Heavenly Father.' The words of the Redeemer to Peter are well known to us. 'Amen, amen, I say to you, the cock will not crow before you deny me three times' (Jn 13,38).

"And so it happened. But when in the house of the priest, the cock crowed, Jesus looked at Peter. Peter remembered the words the Lord told him... "'he went out and began to weep bitterly' (Lk 22,61-62). These were tears of grief, tears of conversion which confirmed the truth of his confession. Due to them, after the resurrection, he could say to Jesus: 'Lord, you know everything: you know that I love you.'

"Today, here in Syracuse, I have the joy to consecrate the Shrine of Our Lady of Tears. I hear, resounding in me today, in this place, the words Christ said to Peter: 'And so I say to you, you are Peter, and upon this rock I will build My Church, and the gates of the netherworld shall not prevail against it. I shall give you the keys to the kingdom of Heaven. Whatever you bind on earth shall be bound in Heaven; and whatever you loose on earth shall be loosed in Heaven' (Mt 16, 18-19).

"These words of Christ express the supreme authority which He, as Redeemer, possesses: the power to forgive sins, obtained at the price of the blood shed on Golgotha; the power to absolve and to forgive.

"Oh, Shrine of the Virgin Mary of Tears, you have risen to remind the Church of the tears of the Mother.

"It also reminds us of the tears of Peter to whom Christ has entrusted the keys of the Kingdom of Heaven, for the good of all the faithful. May these keys serve to bind and loose for the redemption of every human misery.

"Here, within the welcoming walls, come those who are oppressed with the awareness, of sin, and may they experience here, the riches of the mercy of God and of His forgiveness! They are guided here by the tears of the Mother.

"They are tears of grief for those who refuse the love of God, for the broken families or families in difficulties, for the youth oppressed by the civilization of consumerism, and often disoriented by the violence that causes so much bloodshed, for the misunderstanding and hatred which dig out a profound division between men and nations.

"They are tears of prayer: prayer of the Mother, which gives strength to any other prayer, and rises beseechingly also for those who do not pray, because they are absorbed by thousands of interests and because they are firmly closed to the call of God.

"They are tears of hope, which melt

the hardness of hearts and open them to the encounter with Christ the Redeemer, source of light and peace for each one, the families and the entire society.

"The Mother of Tears looks with motherly goodness to the sorrows of the world! She wipes away the tears of those who suffer, of those who are forgotten, of those in despair, of the victims of violence.

"Oh Mother, grant us tears of repentance and of new life, which open the hearts to the regenerating gift of the love of God. Grant us all tears of joy, after having seen the profound kindness of Your heart. Blessed be God!"

(From the homily of the Holy Father during the Eucharistic Celebration for the dedication of the Shrine of the Mother of Tears on June 11, 1994.)

WHY THE VIRGIN MARY SHEDS TEARS

Mary told a victim-soul the reason why She sheds tears: "My tears of blood in Italy and in the world are a gentle reminder for all My children. I still come to you, I cry for you, but you are not listening to Me. Rather, these My tears are scorned and trampled under foot by the great majority.

"Do not complain if then punishment comes. God is good and merciful and He still allows Me to come to you, but the time of Divine Justice is near.

"I am still interceding before the throne of the Most High because I want you all to be saved, give Me your sufferings and prayers to save humanity. There is still a little time left."

MARY'S MESSAGE

December 25, 1995

"Glorify the Father with Me. My children, I give you thanks because you have stayed with Me during this time of grace which leads to eternity.

"It is I who am passing through the world and knock at the door of many hearts. I try to save what has still remained uncontaminated, and to call all My children back to conversion.

"Do not reject the grace I am giving. Do not waste time listening to the world which is pursuing a monstrous project: the one of substituting himself for God the Creator.

"My children, it is necessary to live in the greatest holiness to resist and be ready, because the time of God's visitation is very near. All of you come close to me to be able to live everyday this day which initiates salvation.

"Dear children, with my blessing I enclose all of you in my immense love."

OUR LADY'S REQUEST AT KRUSHIV

Our Lady appeared at Krushiv in Ukrania on August 26, 1987. Eleven-year-old Marina Kyzyn was the first to see Mary on the top of the church tower of an abandoned chapel, behind her home. Many people saw the apparition which lasted several days. Josyp Terelya, visionary of the Ukranian Catholics, affirms:

"Light was coming from the dome spreading all over. I saw a woman in the light looking at me and giving me courage. 'How beautiful,' I thought. It was a supernatural face and at the same time human and familiar. I saw Her daily during my ten days stay in the region.

"THE VIRGIN MARY WAS CRYING AND ASKING FOR PENANCE FOR THE FORGIVENESS OF SINS."